think

like a pony

on the ground

STEP 3 WORKBOOK

Lynn Henry

KENILWORTH PRESS

Illustrated by Su Smith
Photography by Rachael Lynch
Design by Vikki Hirst

Published in Great Britain in 2007 by
Kenilworth Press, an imprint of Quiller Publishing Ltd

British Library Cataloguing in Publication Data
A catalogue record for this book is available from the
British Library

ISBN 978-1-905693-12-2

Printed in China

KENILWORTH PRESS
An imprint of Quiller Publishing Ltd
Wykey House, Wykey, Shrewsbury, SY4 1JA
tel: 01939 261616 fax: 01939 261606
e-mail: info@quillerbooks.com
website: www.kenilworthpress.co.uk

Acknowledgments

I would like to thank my friends for the
important part they have played in helping
me to produce these books.

Thank you to Su Smith for your wonderful
illustrations, which capture the
imagination of children and adults alike.

Thank you to Rachael Lynch for your
wonderful photography. Working with
animals and children is not easy.

Thank you to Su Cliff for your precise
editing, without you I would never have
had the courage to produce these books.

Thank you to Vikki Hirst – designing these
workbooks has truly brought out the child
in you!

Thank you to all the children and ponies
who have inspired me to complete these
books.

think
like a pony
on the ground
STEP 3 WORKBOOK

Contents

ABOUT THE AUTHOR

Lynn Henry is an instructor of horsemanship, both on the ground and ridden. She lives in West Yorkshire, England, with her husband and four children.

A dedicated senior school teacher before leaving to bring up her family of three boys and a girl, Lynn has had a lifelong passion for teaching and particularly the teaching of children.

Lynn came to the horse world relatively late in life (thirty-five) as a result of helping her children to learn about ponies and riding and was immediately captivated by the relationship between human and pony. She has since dedicated fourteen years to horse psychology, with particular emphasis on building a strong foundation on which to develop better understanding, harmony and friendship between pony and student.

Forever in pursuit of a holistic approach to horses, Lynn has added shiatsu for horses and iridology for horses to her list of ever-widening skills.

FOREWORD
by Carl Hester

When Lynn Henry asked me to write the foreword for this book I was delighted to be able to add my thoughts to what is a very special introduction to handling horses and ponies on the ground. When I was young I lived on Sark in the Channel Islands and I had a very special friend called Jacko – who wasn't a pony but a donkey. Life in those days was a carefree existence and I learned all my horsemanship skills through trial and error with the horses on Sark and dear old Jacko. I didn't have a book like this to help me understand why ponies act the way they do and how to work with them in a safe way.

I have five godchildren – all boys – and this book is ideal for them. Even if they decide they don't want to follow my steps into dressage they will at least have a great knowledge of ponies – which can be dangerous to be around or ride if you don't understand them and they don't understand you.

If you dream of having the perfect pony who stands still while you get on, doesn't barge you out of the way to get to his field and would never dream of biting you, then you need to learn the language of ponies. This great book is easy to understand and is a must for any boy or girl who wants to be around horses and ponies. It is also great for non-horsy parents and will teach them a thing or two as well!

CARL HESTER

Introduction

It is important that parents and children have read and understood the Step 1 and Step 2 Workbooks before starting to work through Step 3.

The aim of this book is to build on the knowledge and skills outlined in Step 1 and Step 2.

This book explains how these skills are based on a language that ponies use with each other.

You will better understand the importance of personal space and body language.

You will learn to develop a language on the ground that a pony can understand, then use this language to communicate with him. This way a pony can understand what is being asked of him and learn to make the correct response.

Through simple exercises without a pony, you are prepared to work through exercises with a pony.

You will learn to develop empathy with a pony through simulation exercises, developing a better understanding of how a pony moves.

By developing a language and skills on the ground, a pony will see you as a leader who he can respect, trust and feel safe with.

You are asked to develop a feel when working with a pony, so that when you direct a pony's movement it will be light. This helps you to be confident and feel safe around a pony.

Being able to direct a pony's feet easily allows you to carry out simple tasks safely, for example:

- **leading**
- **asking a pony to move in or out of a stable or through a gate**
- **picking up his feet**
- **preparing a pony to jump or negotiate an obstacle**

This ability to direct a pony's feet from the ground is essential preparation for ridden work.

All the workbooks in this series use simple language, photographs and illustrations to explain how to achieve this. The lessons are progressive and sequential, each building on the last.

This way skills and understanding are developed slowly so that they become permanent.

You will learn to watch a pony's body language, to understand his feelings and to listen to what he is saying. **This way you can build a relationship with a pony; you can become willing partners together and be safe with each other. You can become friends!**

Chapter 1
Follow your nose

Your pony needs to be flexible so that he can use his body freely and enjoy moving. When he is flexible and can move freely, he will then be easier to handle and ride. He will have little resistance when you are asking him to manoeuvre.

What about you?
Have you ever thought about being flexible? What does this mean?

How freely does your body move? Can you:
1. Bend?
2. Stretch?
3. Turn?
4. Move in different directions?

How does it feel to be inflexible?

When your body becomes inflexible it can cause discomfort and pain. If you hurt a muscle or damage a bone or joint, it can cause you to be stiff and uncomfortable.

The best thing to increase flexibility is correct exercises. These can stretch your muscles and flex your joints. When your muscles hurt it makes them feel better if you rub them (give them a massage).

If your pony is not flexible, he will not be able to follow his nose on a circle. He will look uncomfortable and out of balance.

think
like a pony
on the ground

You and your pony have very similar bodies – you are both mammals, you have a skeleton made of bones and it is covered with muscles and skin.

You use two of your limbs (your legs) to stand up on.

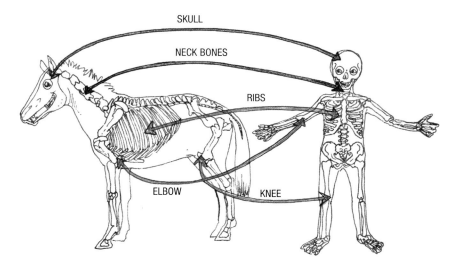

SKULL

NECK BONES

RIBS

ELBOW   KNEE

Your pony uses four limbs to stand up on.

Did you know that both you and your pony have seven vertebrae (bones) in your neck?

One of the best exercises to help your pony to become more flexible is to move his body on a circle.

This helps him to:
1. Bend his body.
2. Stretch over his back and neck.
3. Use his joints.
4. Find a rhythm.

When your pony moves his body on a circle to the left, he stretches and uses the right side of his body more.

think
like a pony
on the ground

When he moves his body on a circle to the right, he then stretches the other side of his body.

To keep his body flexible on both sides it is important that he moves his body on a circle in both directions.

To understand how it feels to move your body in a circle you are going to pretend to be a pony.

Try this! Moving like a pony

1. Kneel down on the floor as if you were a pony, with your legs hip-width apart and your arms shoulder-width apart. Your arms should be underneath your shoulders, not out in front of you. With your weight even on your hands and knees, let your head follow your neck.

2. Look straight down at the floor and relax your head and neck; imagine your neck is your pony's neck. Keep your weight a little bit backwards on your knees; keep your back straight but soft.

think
like a pony
on the ground

3. Now turn your nose, and your head and neck, a little to the left and look over your left hand. Wait to feel the sensations in your body.

Is there any weight shift? Your weight should be in your right hand.

If you were to start moving, in which direction would you move – to the left or the right?

You will naturally want to go to the left.

4. Now turn your nose, head, neck and shoulder a little to the left. As you do, notice what happens in the rest of your body.

Where do your hips go? Your hips should move to the right. What happens to your weight in your hands and knees?

Your hips move as your shoulders move and your weight moves to the right-hand knee.

5. With your nose and shoulders turned to the left, try to pick up your left hand. Make sure you don't rock forwards.

6. Without adjusting your weight try to pick up your right hand.

Which is easier?

It is easier to pick up your left hand.

If you cannot feel this, check that you are not leaning to the left or rocking forwards.

In this position, where do you feel a bend in your body? Where did you feel a stretch in your body?

You should feel a bend on your left side and a stretch on your right side.

When you are doing these exercises try to think like a pony.

7. Repeat the exercise but this time look to the right.

Are you more flexible to the left, or to the right?

Does it feel same on both sides?

As your body turns and moves your weight shifts.

Now you have an understanding of how your pony feels as he begins to turn in a circle.

To move in the circle you should try to maintain this bend in your body and follow your nose forward.

Try this! Following your nose on a circle

1. Take up a position on your hands and knees with your weight a little bit backwards and your back soft.

2. Turn your nose, head and shoulder to look over your left hand.

As you turn your nose, head and shoulders you should feel your weight shift into your right hand and knee.

3. Pick up your left hand and lift it out and forward onto a circle. Keep looking to the left and turn your shoulders over your left hand.

think
like a pony
on the ground

4. Pick up your right leg and step it forward.

Now your weight has shifted, so you are free to pick up your right hand and move it forward on to the circle. Maintain your body position.

5. Pick up your left leg and bring it forward on to the circle.

Now your body position should have a bend to the left and a stretch to the right.

This is how your pony should move on a circle and this is the sequence of his footfalls when he walks to the left.

Walk

① ③
④ ②

If he were to trot, the bend and stretch would be the same but his footfalls sequence would be different. In trot he moves two feet at once in diagonal pairs.

Trot

① ②
② ①

If he were to canter the bend and stretch would be the same but his footfalls sequences would be different.

Canter

To keep your pony's body flexible and moving freely, it is IMPORTANT that:
1. His nose leads.
2. His neck and shoulder follow.
3. His ribs follow.
4. His hips follow.

Your pony's legs can position themselves underneath him so they can flex and push him along easily.

If your pony is not allowed to follow his nose, or cannot follow his nose because he is stiff and uncomfortable, he will not be able to move on a circle correctly.

Now try this!

1. Take up your 'pony position' on your hands and knees, on the floor.

2. Turn your nose and head to the right to look over your right hand.

3. Now with your nose and head looking to the right start to move out on a circle to the left.

4. Move one limb at a time: hand, leg, hand, leg

5. Make at least two sequences

Is it difficult to stay on the circle or are you forced straight?

Can your legs follow easily or do they get confused?

think
like a pony
on the ground

6. Now turn your nose, head and shoulders to the right and try to walk like a pony on a circle again.

Has it now become more difficult?

How do you think this would feel for your pony if he was moving like this?

REMEMBER! **To move freely, the nose leads the neck and the shoulders follow, then the ribs and hips.**

Your body naturally wants to follow your nose, so where your nose points the rest of the body will naturally want to go. It feels very strange to point your nose in one direction and then move the other way. You have to think about it.

Some ponies are stiff and inflexible. They may be sore in their muscles, bones or joints. They will find moving on a circle difficult and may have forgotten how to move freely. They will feel 'stuck' and unable to follow their nose.

Ponies do not understand that moving correctly on a circle can help them to become flexible and move freely.

It is IMPORTANT **to slowly introduce your pony to moving on a circle so he can have time to feel and think about his experience. If his muscles are tight and stiff, he will need time to let go and relax.**

The more he moves freely on a circle, the more he will enjoy his body and become more flexible and strong. He needs to be flexible and strong if you are going to ride him.

Chapter 2
Asking your pony to move out onto a circle

You are going to use what you have learned so far to help your pony to follow his nose and move his body on a circle. This can be difficult for both of you at first, so you are going to do the exercise in stages.

You must be very clear with your steady feel and signals so your pony can make sense of what you are asking. This is why you will first practise this without your pony.

Ask a friend to be the pony. You will be the handler.

Make sure you both understand that the handler is going to direct the pony out onto a circle.

Try this! Directing your pony onto a circle

Circle to the right.

1. Have the halter with the rope attached.

2. Ask your friend to hold the halter by the nose knots and put their hands straight out in front of them. Your friend's hands are acting as your pony's head and their arms as his neck.

3. Stand facing each other and put your hand out so you cannot touch each other's hand.

4. Hold the rope attached to the halter about an arm's length from the snap in your right hand. Let the snap hang down in neutral.

5. Hold the tail end of the rope about an arm's length from the end.

6. Allow the middle of the rope to hang in front of your body. (If there is too much rope looping in the middle, take a step away from your partner and lengthen the rope attached to the halter.)

7. Still looking at your partner with soft eyes, lift your arm holding the rope attached to the halter and point out onto a circle away from you.

Your partner must understand not to come forward and into your personal space. Your feel on the rope gives direction as to where you would like them to step. To feel this steady pressure clearly, the rope must not be too long.

8. Think about directing your partner out and away, just as you would point to show someone the way.

You would not pull them, you would show them!

To help your pony follow the feel of the rope easily, you will need to adjust his weight backwards to free up his front legs.

If you have the rope attached to the halter in your right hand, then you are asking your pony right. You will need to free up the front leg that he will use to step out onto the circle. If he is going on a right circle, this will be his left leg.

9. Stand in front of your partner and ask them to take a backward step. You can use rhythmic or steady pressure to do this. Ask them to take a backward step until the weight is on their right foot. Ask them to stay there. When the left leg is free and ready to move, lift up the rope attached to the halter and direct them onto a circle.

You may need to talk this through and try the manoeuvre several times.

think
like a pony
on the ground

10. Your partner should feel it easier to step out onto the circle when they have time to adjust their weight. This frees up their left leg to be able to step out.

Compare what it feels like when you direct them out onto a circle without adjusting their weight.

Which did they prefer?

When you adjust your pony's weight like this before you ask him to take a step, he will be more willing to follow your feel and move out onto a circle.

If he does not understand you, then you will have to support your feel of steady pressure on the rope with rhythmic pressure from your other hand, twirling the rope or stick.

When a policeman is directing traffic he points to where he wants the traffic to go, then waves his arm to encourage the cars along.

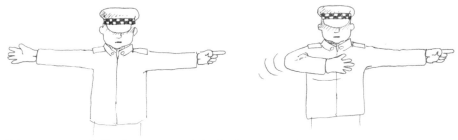

When you use rhythmic pressure, it is the front end of your pony, the part in front of the drive line, that you are encouraging to move out onto a circle — like a policeman directing traffic.

11. Ask your partner to back up and free their left leg. When you lift your arm to ask them out onto a circle, ask them to ignore your feel.

12. Now lift your left arm holding the free end of the rope out by your side to shoulder height and wait. This will give your partner time to see this new signal.

13. Now take your arm towards their outstretched arms (this is like your pony's neck). Maintain the feel on the rope attached to the halter so your partner feels they are being directed out onto a circle. Wait so they can see this new signal.

14. Now, using circular motion of your arm, increase the signal by putting rhythm in your arm or rope.

15. Using a circular movement tap them gently on their arm. Maintain the feel on the rope attached to the halter directing them out onto a circle.

You may need to take a step forward to tap them on the arm.

16. As soon as your partner steps out onto the circle **ALLOW** them to move by letting the rope attached to the halter slip through your fingers. At the same time turn with them, looking at their head.

It is IMPORTANT that you repeat this exercise many times so that you can remember the sequence of steady pressure followed by rhythmic pressure before you do this with your pony.

It is **IMPORTANT** that your partner sees your signals:
1. Lift your hand holding the rope attached to the halter.
2. Lift out your free hand.
3. Point towards their outstretched arms.
4. Twirl your rope towards their arms.

Then **ALLOW** them to move by letting the rope slip through your hand and turn with them.

think
like a pony
on the ground

Later, when you are with your pony, you will:

1. Lift your arm holding the rope attached to the halter. This gives a feel of steady pressure for your pony to follow.

2. Then you point to his neck.

3. Then you twirl towards his neck.

4. Then you touch or tap his neck.

Just like a policeman directing traffic!

When your pony is moving on a circle, you must allow the rope to slip through your hands and turn with him. If you do not allow the rope to slip through your hands, you will cause your pony to stop.

When you want your pony to stop and look at you, you will ask him to move his hindquarters and turn to face you.

Try this! Moving the pony out onto a circle and back to you

1. Ask your partner to move out onto a circle and do not let the rope slip through your hands. Keep your hands closed and tight.

Your partner will feel they want to stop and come close to you.

Ask them to move out on a circle again, and this time do not turn with them. Ask them how this feels.

They will feel they cannot move.

2. Now ask your partner to walk out onto a circle again. Try to turn on the spot or walk a small circle as you watch your partner walk on a bigger circle. Follow them on the circle. Keep your hand and your belly button lined up with their hands. While you turn, keep your body upright and relaxed and your eyes soft.

3. Allow the rope attached to the halter to slip slowly out of your hand. As you do, maintain a forward feel on the rope.

4. Hold the rope towards the end lightly to stop it slipping out of your hand. This will hold your partner out on a circle that is the rope's length away from you.

5. Keep your hand and belly button lined up with your partner's nose as you turn on the spot. Ask your partner to keep their hands out in front of them and relax.

You are now going to get ready to ask your partner to turn and look at you and to stop.

Change your focus and your intention. Imagine that your pony is going to turn and look at you. To do this he will step his hindquarters away from you; this will cause him to turn.

Stop looking at his front end and focus on his back end. This is his first signal that you are asking him to do something different.

6. Now take the rope nearest the halter in both hands. Turn your right hand over, fingers on top, and place your knuckles on top of the rope. Slide your hand down as far as you can reach. This will cause you to change your body language.

Your partner should feel you reach down the rope and be aware of your new body position. Your partner should feel this and want to turn to you.

think
like a pony
on the ground

7. As you start to reach down the rope, walk towards your partner's bottom (as if it were the rear end of your pony) and have the intention that you would like them to move their bottom away from you and turn to face you. This will cause them to stop.

8. Maintain your new feel on the rope; this will give your partner the feel to come to you. Maintain your body position. Keep walking towards their bottom.

Your partner should feel as if they want to turn to face you.

9. To show your partner you want them to stop outside your personal space stand up to signal to them.

Now repeat the exercise asking your partner to go to the left.

11. Circle to the left.

12. Now start again but this time hold the rope nearest the halter in your left hand.

13. Ask your partner to take a backward step and put their weight in their left foot. When their right foot is free ask them to step onto a circle to the left.

14. When you want them to look back at you, look at their rear end, run your left hand down the rope towards the halter. Walk towards their bottom.

think
like a pony
on the ground

When your partner is walking on a circle and you want them to look at you and stop, the feel on the rope should be suggesting that you want them to follow the feel and look at you.

Walking towards their bottom and having the intention you want them to step away causes them to turn to you.

If you pull your partner to you they feel as if they are unbalanced and falling into you.

Experiment with this and try pulling your partner onto the circle to look at you without at first looking at their bottom or running your hand down the rope. Ask them how this feels.

If you walk backwards when your partner is moving on a circle, they will feel you are asking them to come closer to you. Try it!

Repeat the exercise several times until you feel comfortable with the techniques.

When you ask your pony to walk on a circle you can think about:
1. Asking him to step out.
2. Allowing him to walk on the circle.
3. Asking him to look back at you.

When you have tried this a few times swap over so you are the pony.

This way you can feel what it is like to be a pony and a handler.

It is IMPORTANT you get a feel of these techniques before you try this with your pony.

Your pony may not be as co-operative as your human partner.

Chapter 3
Onto a circle and back again

Imagine a ballerina standing on a musical box – she turns on the spot.

That is how you are going to turn with your pony so you can use soft eyes to look at him. When you look at him you can be aware of how he is moving on the circle.

Is he looking out of the circle?

Is his back end following his front end?

Does he look comfortable on the circle?

If he is moving correctly on a circle:
1. His front legs and shoulders should follow his nose and neck.
2. His hind legs and hips should follow his ribs, shoulders and front legs.
3. He should look like he is on a track.

think
like a pony
on the ground

When you look at your pony you are trying to support him and encourage him with your attitude to stay out on the circle. You want him to be aware of you but not be frightened by you.

You are his friend helping him to move on a circle. Later, moving freely on a circle will help him relax his body, be flexible and strong and easier to ride.

When you have practised asking your partner out onto a circle and you are confident that you can repeat these techniques with your pony you are ready to ask your pony to step onto a circle.

When he has walked half a circle you are going to ask him to look at you. You are going to do this by pushing his hindquarters away from you and drawing the front end to you.

You will draw the front end of your pony to you using **steady pressure**.

You will push his hindquarters away using your **body language and rhythmic signals of pressure**.

Your pony will then feel you are asking him to turn to you.

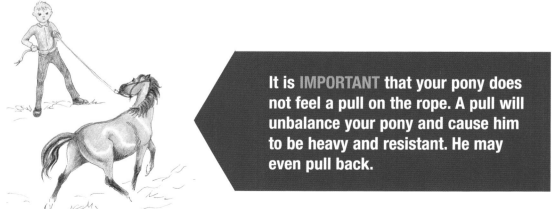

It is IMPORTANT that your pony does not feel a pull on the rope. A pull will unbalance your pony and cause him to be heavy and resistant. He may even pull back.

As you practise these techniques you will find your pony turns to face you from a very light feel on the rope and a look from you towards his hindquarters.

When he steps out onto to a circle allow the rope to slip through your hands. He may only take up half the rope and move onto a circle closer to you or he may walk out onto a bigger circle. It does not matter at this time.

You must keep turning with him, making sure you are allowing him to move. Your hand holding the rope attached to the halter should show him the way with a feel of 'go forwards'.

Exercise 1 – Asking your pony out onto a circle

With adult supervision, in a safe place where you and your pony feel comfortable, put the halter on and have the rope attached. Ensure there is enough room so you can ask your pony to walk at the end of the rope.

1. Stand in front of your pony with the rope over your arm or holding it in your hands. Give him a friendly rub.

think
like a pony
on the ground

2. Ask him to take a step away from you so you can just touch his nose. You can ask him to back away from you using steady pressure on the fiador knot or rhythmical signals of pressure from your foot or rope. Make sure the snap is in neutral when you use rhythmic signals of pressure.

3. You are going to ask your pony to step out onto a right circle. To do this you must hold the rope attached to the halter in your right hand, hold the free end of the rope in your other hand about an arm's length from the end. Ask your pony to look at you with two eyes. If you need to, use steady pressure on the halter and ask him to look left or right until he looks at you.

When he looks at you with two eyes, he is giving you his attention and he is not thinking about escaping left or right. Give him a reason to look at you, be gentle in your attitude but positive in your feel. Rub him in between his eyes when he looks at you.

Make sure the length of rope attached to the halter is about an arm's length and the snap is in neutral. This way when you lift the rope to direct your pony's feet he will be able to feel what you are asking him to do.

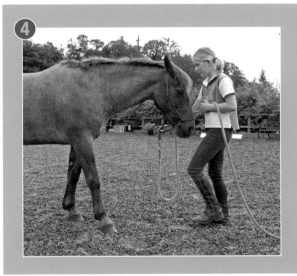

4. Ask your pony to take a step backwards so he can shift his weight off his front legs. Back him up until his weight is back and over his right front leg and his left front leg is free.

5. Now it is possible for him to lift his left leg out to a circle. Make sure his weight stays back. If his weight comes forward he will not step to the side but will step towards you.

think
like a pony
on the ground

6. Lift your right arm up and out to the side and point in the direction that you want him to go. This puts a feel through the rope to the halter that your pony can follow out to a circle.

7. If your pony steps out and walks forward onto a circle, allow the rope to slip through your hand so your pony feels he can move.

As he moves you should turn with him, standing in your personal space, turning on the spot like a toy ballerina on a musical box.

Keep your eyes in line with his face, your belly button in line with his nose and your hand allowing him forward and showing him the way.

As you watch him keep your eyes soft and be aware of his whole body. You should still be able to see his tail and should be aware of where he is going and where he has been.

8. When he has walked about half a circle you are going to ask him to look at you. Look at his hindquarters. This changes your body language and it is the first thing he will see. Keep looking at his bottom, turn your hand so your knuckles are on top, and slide your hand nearest his head down the rope towards the halter.

This will cause your body language to change and your pony will see it. Have the feel that you want to keep your hand holding the rope attached to the halter near to your belly button. Make sure you do not pull the rope and your pony to you. Try to keep your hands open and soft. It is OK to close your hand if your pony pulls against you.

With your hand in this position your pony will feel a gentle steady pressure on the halter that will ask him to come to you.

9. With your hand in this position, still looking at his bottom, start to walk towards his hindquarters.

Have the intention that his hindquarters are going to move out of your way. If his hindquarters do not move, use rhythmic signals of pressure to support your feel of gentle steady pressure through the rope, your body language and intention.

This rhythmic pressure could be:
A. A twirl of the rope towards his hindquarters as you walk towards him.
B. A slap on your leg with your hand.
C. Lifting your rope and bobbing it up and down.

10. When your pony understands that you want him to look at you he will try to stop. He will cross his back leg underneath him and try to look at you.

think
like a pony
on the ground

This may take time and you must be willing to keep walking towards his bottom, at the same time holding the rope attached to the halter near to your belly button, making sure you are not pulling on his head.

When he stops, reward him by giving him praise and a big rub. If your pony takes a long time to step his hindquarters away and look at you, slide your hand down the rope attached to the halter. This will give him a stronger feel to come to you.

If your pony does not want to step out onto the circle . . .

Your pony may need help to follow the feel of the rope onto a circle.

If he does not want to step out correctly but tries to walk over to you he may be confused or stubborn, it does not matter which. It is your job to communicate clearly what you are asking him to do.

Make sure his weight is back and in the correct leg so that he can step out freely.

Make sure the feel on the rope attached to the halter is directing him out and forward onto a circle, not towards you.

If both these things are in place then you will need to support the feel of steady pressure on the rope with rhythmic signals of pressure.

Exercise 2 – Using rhythmic pressure to support your steady feel to ask your pony to step into a circle.

1. Stand in front of your pony. Hold the rope attached to the halter in your right hand and the other free end in your left hand, about an arm's length from the end. Make sure the snap is in neutral.

2. Ask your pony to politely and slowly step away from you so he is just outside your personal space. You can use either steady pressure or rhythmical pressure to do this.

3. Ask him to look at you with two eyes. Be gentle and polite about this – take your time. If he comes forward, ask him politely to step back and keep your feet still.

4. When you are both ready ask your pony to shift his weight back to free up his front left leg.

5. When this happens lift up your hand holding the rope attached to the halter and direct your pony out onto a circle.

Make sure you do not pull him forwards.

6. If he does not step out, lift up your hand and arm holding the free end of your rope straight out from your side.

This makes your body language bigger.

Keep looking at your pony and hold the feel on the rope attached to the halter, directing your pony out onto a circle.

think
like a pony
on the ground

7. If your pony does not step out onto a circle, bring your arm across towards his shoulder or neck.

Keep looking at him and maintain the feel on the rope to direct him out onto a circle. If he steps out allow the rope to slip through your hands so he can move.

8. If he does not step out start to twirl the rope towards his neck.

This increases the rhythmic pressure and gives your pony a clear message that you want him to move away from you onto a circle. As soon as he takes a step away from you stop twirling and allow him to move. If he steps out, allow the rope to slip through your hands so he can move.

9. If he does not step out you will have to let the rope touch him on the neck. Keep looking at him and maintain the feel.

As soon as he steps away from you, stop twirling and let the rope slip through your hands, allowing him to step onto the circle.

The length of rope that you use to twirl will depend on your height and the distance your pony is from you. Experiment with this and be ready to adjust to fit yourself and your pony. If you and your pony are small you may only need to twirl your hand and tap him with your hand and not use the rope.

Some ponies may become confused, not understanding what you are asking, and start to back away from you. They may look tense and frightened.

If this happens to you make sure you are directing your pony out onto a circle with your hand holding the rope attached to the halter so he can feel where you want him to go.

If your pony backs away from you, you will have to walk with him. Try to maintain the distance away from him that you started with.

Make sure your feel on the rope attached to the halter is showing him where to go. Support your direct feel with rhythmic signals of pressure towards his front end (in front of the drive line). As soon as he steps out, stop and reward him. Give him plenty of time to think. He has found this difficult! Make sure you do not speed up or ask too much. Give your pony time to think and work out what you are asking. Look for body language signs that let you know he is thinking and understanding. As he starts to understand what you want he will start to relax.

think
like a pony
on the ground

If you find twirling the rope difficult...
...then try to direct your pony out on to a circle using your arm like a policeman to show him where you want to go.

If your pony trots on a circle...
...that is OK, just keep following the instructions and work through the exercise.

If your pony acts dangerously...
...at any time and threatens you, seek professional help.

If your pony stops on the circle . . .

When your pony is on a circle, as you turn with him you can show him, through the feel down the line to the halter, that you want him to go forward.

If he stops you can support this feel by putting your arm out and imagine you can reach behind him.

If he does not follow this feel and suggestion...
...you can show him you want him to go forwards by adding rhythmic signals of pressure behind him. This will suggest to him that you want him to go forward.

think
like a pony
on the ground

Exercise 3 – Using rhythmic signals of pressure behind your pony to ask him to go forward

1. With a forward feel on the halter, lift your free hand straight out by your side. This makes your body language bigger. Now start to swirl your arm to put rhythm out behind your pony's bottom.

If he moves forward, stop twirling.

If he does not move forward, maintain the forward feel on the halter. Slap your hand against your leg with rhythm until he does walk forward.

When he does walk forward, stop slapping and tell him he is a good boy and turn with him.

2. If you have enough rope you can use the end of your rope in your free hand. Twirling the rope will increase your body language.

think
like a pony
on the ground

Lift your arm holding the free end of the rope. If your pony does not move forward, twirl the rope to put rhythmic pressure behind him. Keep twirling your rope and maintain a forward feel on the halter until he goes forward.

Some ponies might trot forward on the circle – that is OK, just keep following the exercise.

REMEMBER! When you want him to go forward you need to put pressure behind the drive line.

If your pony stops on the circle and looks at you…
If your pony stops on the circle and looks at you, his front feet have come off the circle.

The first thing you must do is put his front feet back on the circle.

When his front feet are back on the circle you can ask him to move forward and the rest of his body will follow.

When he stops and looks at you and you have not asked him to, then start again. Ask him to move his weight so you can direct him back onto a circle as you did in the first exercise.

If he keeps stopping and looking at you make sure:

• The feel on the halter is asking him forward.

• You are turning with him, your eyes looking at his, your belly button lined up with the rope and snap.

• You are not pulling the rope attached to the halter towards you and you are allowing him to move forward.

If you have checked all this then watch for the moment he starts to look at you. This may be just a twitch of his ear, or his eye will turn to look at you.

think
like a pony
on the ground

It is a signal that he may be thinking about stopping and turning off the circle to look at you. This is the time to give him a stronger feel to go forwards on the circle and suggest with your free hand that he follows the feel to go forward by putting rhythmic pressure behind his bottom.

If he still looks like he is going to turn toward you then bring your hand towards his neck, suggesting he stay out.

If you can, you may want to twirl your rope towards his neck to move his front end away on to the circle.

REMEMBER! **Rhythmical signals of pressure suggest he follows your feel of steady pressure on the halter.**

Making the circle bigger

Your pony needs space to be able to use his body freely, and to do this he needs to make the circle as big as possible.

If you stand in your personal space, your pony's circle is going to be 9–10 feet (3m) in diameter.

If you do not allow the rope to move through your hand and hold it towards the end, then you will be making his circle smaller.

Sometimes your pony will make the circle smaller himself, either because he is not confident at a distance from you, or he is not comfortable moving on a circle.

think
like a pony
on the ground

It is IMPORTANT that your pony is confident and comfortable making a circle around you.

If he can walk, trot and (later) canter on a circle by himself then he can move easily and maintain a circle comfortably when you ride him.

If your pony does not take the circle to the end of the rope then you will have to show him what you want him to do.

Exercise 4 – Asking your pony to go to the end of the rope

With your pony on a circle, hold the free end of the rope in your free hand.

Maintain the forward feel on the rope attached to the halter.

Now use rhythmic pressure towards the front end of your pony.

Rhythmic signals of pressure here will send the front end away and out onto the circle.

1. Put rhythmic signals of pressure in the free end of the rope by twirling or swinging it towards the front end of your pony in front of the drive line.

It is IMPORTANT that the rhythmic pressure stays in front of the drive line so your pony knows which bit of him you are talking to and trying to move.

2. As your pony moves away from you, allow the rope to slip and move through your hand so he can move onto a bigger circle.

If he trots, do not worry. Just keep working through the exercise.

think
like a pony
on the ground

3. Keep turning with him. When he has walked at least one complete circle around you, ask him to move his hindquarters away using rhythmic signals of pressure and look at you using steady pressure on the halter.

Exercise 5 – Using a stick to make your body language bigger

Your body language must always be clear to your pony so he can see your signals.

If he can see your signals clearly he is more likely to understand what you are asking.

If he understands what you are asking he is more likely to do what you ask!

Using a stick makes you bigger so you can more easily direct or touch your pony.

You can use a stick just the same as a twirling rope to suggest that your pony follows your feel on the halter.

think
like a pony
on the ground

You can touch your pony with rhythmic pressure to suggest that he steps his front end away from you onto the circle.

You can use your stick and direct the rhythmic pressure at his hindquarters to suggest he moves his bottom away from you.

Make sure you keep your feel of steady pressure on the rope attached to the halter so that your pony can feel what you want him to do.

You can rub your pony with your stick to say 'thank you'.

If you are small and your pony is small, twirling your arm may be enough to increase your signal. If you are a little bigger use your stick to increase your signal. Reward your pony often; this way he will know that you care and he will be more willing to do what you ask him.

Chapter 4
Keeping your pony's nose on the circle

Can your pony keep his nose on a circle?

When your pony's nose is on a circle the rest of his body should follow. This helps him to relax his muscles and make him supple.

When he moves on a circle correctly he can:
1. Relax his jaw.
2. Stretch his neck.
3. Free his shoulders.
4. Swing his ribcage and stretch his back.
5. Use his hind legs evenly.
6. Find the rhythm he needs to feel comfortable.

If he circles to the left and then to the right, he stretches and relaxes both sides of his body. To feel this he must be able to follow his nose.

Using the feel of steady pressure on the rope attached to the halter you are going to ask your pony to put his nose onto a circle so the rest of his body can follow.

Exercise 6 – Observing how your pony moves on a circle

Stand in front of your pony and ask him to step out and walk on a circle around you. Turn with him.

Try to get him to the end of the rope. If you need to, use rhythmic signals of pressure to direct him out onto the circle. Turn with him and observe where his nose goes.

When he walks on the circle does he keep his nose:

A. On the circle? **B.** Out of the circle? **C.** Into the middle of the circle?
Do his ribs and shoulders look like they are bulging towards you?

What is the hind end doing?

Is he striding out? In walk a pony's hind feet should step into the footprint that his front feet left. This is called 'tracking up'. If a pony is moving freely and correctly he should overtrack by at least a hoof's length. Is he tracking up? Is he overtracking?

Most ponies turn their noses out of the circle then fall in with their shoulder, coming closer to you and making the circle smaller

Now ask him to face you by suggesting he moves his bottom away from you; use your body language then rhythmic signals of pressure. Keep a steady feel on the rope attached to the halter so he turns to face you.

This time when you ask your pony to walk out on a circle you are going to ask him to keep his nose on the circle and try to keep the same distance from you all the way around.

think
like a pony
on the ground

Exercise 7 – Asking your pony to keep his nose on a circle

1. Ask your pony, using a steady feel on the halter, to walk out on a circle to the right (make sure you rock his weight back and step him out correctly).

2. Turn with him and ask him to go to the end of the rope. Observe where his nose is.

3. When you see his nose poke out of the circle, slide your hand down the rope attached to the halter and ask him, by using a gentle feel of steady pressure, to put his nose back on the circle. Be as gentle as you can. Be careful not to pull. Try to give him the message: 'Please put your nose on the circle.' If you pull on the rope towards yourself your pony may read the message as 'Come to me.'

think
like a pony
on the ground

When you ask him to do this, keep looking at his head, turning with him like a ballerina. This way your pony will know which part you are talking to and that you want him to stay out on the circle. Keep turning with him, keeping your belly button in line with the rope.

 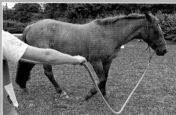 

4. As soon as your pony puts his nose onto the circle release the feel of pressure on the rope attached to the halter.

5. Each time your pony puts his nose out of the circle, reach down the rope and ask him to look onto the circle. When he responds, stop asking. If your pony trots that is OK; just keep following the exercise.

It does not matter if you have to ask 100 times on one circle! You must always release the instant he tries to look onto the circle. This way he knows he is doing the correct thing. He feels the release of pressure when he looks onto the circle.

He will learn it is up to him to keep his nose on the circle. He will not rely on you to keep it there. This is very IMPORTANT when you come to ride him.

6. If your pony stays out on the circle and follows your feel to put his nose on to the circle then he will soon learn that this feels good.

When his body is following his nose he can use his body correctly and relax into the rhythm of his walk, trot or (later) canter.

What if your pony comes closer to you and makes the circle smaller?

If your pony comes closer to you when you ask him to put his nose onto the circle it may be because he thinks that is what you want, or because it is easier for him to fall in.

45

It is IMPORTANT to make sure you are not pulling him towards you, so first check your feel on the rope attached to the halter.

Try sliding your hand down the rope and lifting the rope a little, at the same time slightly tipping your pony's nose in.

This takes practice so be patient with yourself and your pony.

If he stops, move your hand holding the rope attached to the halter forwards, giving him a forward feel. This shows him you want him to keep walking forwards. You may need to encourage him forwards using rhythmic signals of pressure behind the drive line.

If he turns to face you, start again.

If he keeps trying to face you, watch for signs that he is going to stop and look at you and try to encourage the front end to stay out on the circle and moving forward, just as you have done before.

If he is still making the circle smaller, allow him to come closer but keep his nose on the small circle.

Use a stick or the end of your rope to direct rhythmic pressure towards his shoulder. This will give him a signal that you do not want him to come any closer but you want him to move his front end away and try to keep his nose on the circle.

think
like a pony
on the ground

As he responds allow the rope to slip through your hand so he can move out onto a bigger circle.

When you suggest to your pony that he moves his front end away and makes the circle bigger, make sure your rhythmic signals of pressure are gentle. You do not want to frighten him.

It is better that your pony learns to move away slowly. This way he will have time to think, his feet will move rhythmically and his body will not feel confused.

If your pony is very sensitive you may only need to suggest with your body that he moves away from you out onto a bigger circle. You can do this by having the intention in your body that you want him to move away. You could lift up your arms and point to his shoulder and have the feeling you are shooing him away. Make sure you direct your rhythmic signals of pressure in front of the drive line and try to keep his nose on a circle.

You could walk one step towards his shoulder with the intention that you want his front end to move away, at the same time keeping his nose on a circle. It does not matter which signal you use to direct his front end out on to a circle . . .

. . . you will see your pony move a little bit sideways onto a bigger circle.

When your pony puts his nose on the circle allow him to make the circle bigger by letting the rope slip through your hands as you ask his shoulders to move onto a bigger circle. As he moves his shoulders onto a bigger circle the rest of his body follows.

When your pony tries to keep his nose on the circle his body will start to relax.

Reward your pony when he tries to stay on the circle and ask him to stop and look at you. Rub him and say thank you.

Moving on a circle will build up his strength and flexibility. Go slowly so eventually he can walk up to two full circles with his nose leading, his body following.

He does not have to be perfect, just getting a little better each time.

If he looks frightened or anxious you can run your hand down the rope, hold it near your body and push away your pony's hindquarters, using rhythmical signals of pressure until he turns to face you. When he stops give him a rub and start again. When you ask him to keep his nose on the circle see how gentle you can be. Make sure you reward him often.

When you can do this exercise on a circle to the right, repeat it, asking your pony to walk a circle to the left. Does he find going one way easier than the other?
Which way does he prefer?

If you have difficulty keeping your pony in walk on a circle and he keeps breaking into a trot that is OK; continue with the next exercise.

If your pony threatens you or acts dangerously in any way, seek professional help.

When you can ask your pony to keep his nose on a circle in walk, you are ready to ask him to trot on a circle, then keep his nose on a circle while he is trotting.

This is a little harder for him because he is now moving more quickly. It may also be harder for you to learn to follow your pony or use your equipment to ask him to keep his nose on a circle away from you. Take your time. If you need to, go back to asking your pony to walk. When you are both confident you can ask him to trot.

think
like a pony
on the ground

Signs to look for to show he is relaxing and stretching:

1. You will feel him take his nose out of the circle less.
2. He will stay out on the circle.
3. He will drop his head.
4. The way that he trots will look better. It may have a better rhythm or he may lift his feet higher off the ground.
6. He will relax his back.
7. He will swing his back.

It does not matter which sign of relaxation he shows first. Also, you may see more than one.

What is IMPORTANT is that you reward him often and ask him to stop and rest. When he does, give him a big rub and a rest before you ask him to go on a circle again.

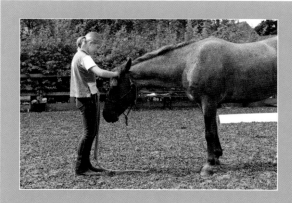

Trotting will cause your pony to stretch and use his body more.

It is IMPORTANT that you look for signs that he is relaxing and trying to keep his nose on the circle, and that you reward him often.

Moving on a circle correctly is tiring so you will need to build his strength and muscles slowly. It may take several circles before you see a sign of relaxation. Be careful not to ask too much of him too soon.

Repeating the exercises once or twice is enough.

think
like a pony
on the ground

Can you ask your pony to trot on a circle?

When your pony feels forward pressure on the halter he knows to go forward.
If he is standing still he should walk.
If he is walking, he should trot.

To ask your pony to follow this forward feel on the halter you may need to encourage him forward by putting rhythmic pressure behind him.

REMEMBER! **Any pressure behind your pony (behind the drive line) will encourage him forward.**

Exercise 8 – Asking your pony to trot on a circle to the right

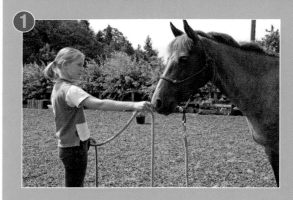

1. Stand in front of your pony and ask him to step out onto a circle to the right, in walk. Turn with him and ask him to go to the end of the rope.

think
like a pony
on the ground

2. When he has travelled about half a circle, lift your hand holding the rope forward. This will give him a feel of forward pressure and is his first signal to trot. Make sure you turn with him keeping your nose with his nose and your belly button lined up with the rope.

This will put your body in to the correct position to show your pony you want him to go forward into trot.

3. If he does not understand to follow the feel of the rope into trot lift your left arm (the hand not holding the rope attached to the halter) out by your side.

This has the effect of making your body language bigger and is a clear signal to your pony that you are asking him to do something. This is his second signal to trot.

Make sure you maintain a forward feel on the rope attached to the halter and keep turning with your pony.

4. If he moves forward into trot put your arm down, allow him to trot forward and turn with him. If he does not trot forward with this signal you will have to put rhythmic signals of pressure behind your pony's drive line. This is his third signal to trot.

You can do this by twirling your arm or twirling the end of your rope.

think
like a pony
on the ground

5. As soon as he moves forward and trots, stop twirling and allow your pony forwards, making sure you turn with him.

When you stop the rhythmic signals of pressure and allow your pony to go forwards he then knows he has done the right thing.

6. If he does not trot forward when you put rhythmic pressure from the twirling rope or hand behind him, you will have to increase the level of rhythmic pressure. To do this you may have to increase the rhythm of your signal or touch your pony with your rope. This is his fourth signal to trot.

7. When your pony has trotted one or two circles around you, prepare to ask him to move his hindquarters away from you, turn to face you and stop.

This is not as easy now that his feet are moving faster.

As you run your hand holding the rope attached to the halter towards his head, have the intention that you would like him to slow down and prepare to stop and look at you.

He will need more time to do this, so go slowly. Make sure your feel is as gentle and polite as possible.

Make sure your body language is clear and look at his hindquarters with your eyes and belly button so that he gets a very clear signal that you are now thinking about his hind end.

Hold the rope in front of your body and be careful not to pull.

think
like a pony
on the ground

Have the intention that you would like his hind end to step away from you and, as it does, your pony will slow down and try to look at you.

Keep walking towards his hindquarters. Using rhythmic pressure if you need to, ask him to move his hindquarters away from you. Be careful not too get too close so that he can still see you and you are not in danger of being kicked.

If your pony finds it difficult to come to a slow stop from trot, you may need to slide your hand nearer to the halter to give him a better feel to come to you.

Keep the rope attached to the halter in front of your body. Keep walking towards his hindquarters and use rhythmic signals of pressure from your hand or rope to ask him to move his hindquarters away from you.

It may feel as if you are both going around in circles. Keep relaxed and hold the intention that you would like him to stop.

Be patient. It WILL happen. If you need to, seek professional help.

When you and your pony are confident about trotting to the right and stopping, then repeat the exercise to the left.

Exercise 9 – Asking your pony to trot on a circle using a stick and string

Some ponies need a bigger signal to ask them to trot forward.

Sometimes a pony may be lazy and unwilling to go forward. Sometimes he may be in pain.

If he is in pain when he trots he will look lame, his stride uneven or he may appear to be limping. Stop working and ask a vet for advice or seek professional help.

If he is lazy you may need to touch him on his bottom with your string.

REMEMBER!

If a young foal does not go forward when his mother asks him to she will bite him on the dock of his tail or on his bottom!

Make sure before you start this task that you have practised using your stick and string.

1. When you want your pony to trot forward use a steady forward feel on the halter.

2. Hold the stick and string in your hand with your arm straight out from your body.

think
like a pony
on the ground

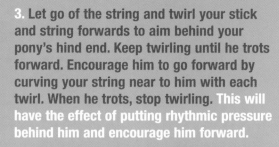

3. Let go of the string and twirl your stick and string forwards to aim behind your pony's hind end. Keep twirling until he trots forward. Encourage him to go forward by curving your string near to him with each twirl. When he trots, stop twirling. **This will have the effect of putting rhythmic pressure behind him and encourage him forward.**

If your pony does not trot forward…

…allow your string to touch him with rhythm.

4. Make sure you put the stick back in front of your body in a neutral position. Then your pony will not feel that you are chasing him with the stick.

It is important that your pony sees the phases of signals:
A. You lift your arm and stick.
B. You twirl your stick and string behind him.
C. You aim your string closer to him.
D. You touch his bottom.

think
like a pony
on the ground

Exercise 10 – Asking your pony to keep his nose on the circle in trot

When your pony is trotting on a circle, turn with him. Ask him, with a feel on the rope attached to the halter, to put his nose on the circle and keep out on the circle.

Follow the instructions as you did in walk to:

A. Keep his nose on a circle. **B.** Move him away from you on a circle.

Look for signs of relaxation and reward him for them.

REMEMBER! You are helping him to become relaxed and supple, strong and athletic. Go slowly and reward your pony often.

Repeat all these exercises on a circle to the left to make sure you work your pony's body equally on both sides.

Chapter 5
Transitions

A transition is a change from one gait to another – for example, from trot to walk, walk to trot, trot to canter or canter to trot.

These transitions are IMPORTANT! **They help your pony to:**
1. Stretch and lift his back.
2. Balance himself.
3. Build muscles.

When your pony feels a backwards pressure on the halter this is a signal to stop going forward.

REMEMBER **pressure directly in front of your pony will ask him to stop and go backwards.**

If a foal gets in front of his mother she will use her body language to signal to him she wants him to be behind her or at the side of her.

You are first going to use steady pressure down the rope to the halter to ask your pony to come down from trot to walk and then go back into trot again. Later, when you ride him, you can use a steady feel of pressure on the rein to ask him to slow down or stop.

Exercise 11 – Asking your pony to come down from trot to walk using steady pressure

With adult supervision, in a safe place where both you and your pony feel comfortable, have the halter on and the rope attached.

1. Stand in front of your pony and ask him with feel to step out onto a circle to the right.

2. Turn with him and ask him to go to the end of the rope. Signal that you want his front end to go away by using rhythm from the end of your rope, your hand or a stick.

3. When your pony is at the end of the rope, lift your hand holding the rope attached to the halter forward. This will give your pony a forward feel and suggest to him that you want him to trot.

If he does not trot, signal to him by putting pressure behind the drive line that you want him to trot. You can use your rhythm from your hand, rope or stick to encourage him forward.

4. Allow him to trot a circle around you. Ask him to keep his nose on a circle. If he comes close to you use rhythmic pressure to ask him to step out onto a bigger circle.

5. Allow him to circle around you and when he tries to keep his nose on a circle and he is not coming into you, then you can ask him to walk.

6. Keep turning with him and run your hand holding the rope attached to the halter backwards so that it puts a backward feel on the halter. Have the intention that you would like him to walk. Keep your body language relaxed.

It is now very IMPORTANT that you keep your belly button and eyes in line with your pony's head. The feel on the rope is asking him to slow down and walk.

think
like a pony
on the ground

If your belly button points to your pony's bottom he will read your body language and think you want him to turn to face you.

REMEMBER! You are trying to teach your pony to read your body language so that you can communicate with him.

7. If your pony does not follow this backward feel to walk, then draw the rope through your hands and walk towards his front end in front of the drive line.

Keep the backward feel on the halter and keep turning with him.

You may need to get closer if he does not understand. This will give him a clear, steady feel through the rope.

Make sure you keep looking at him with your eyes and your belly button. Keep your body relaxed and have the intention that you would like him to walk.

If he turns to face you, encourage him with your hand to keep his nose on the circle.

It may take time for your pony to understand what you are asking.

BE PATIENT! Make sure your feel and intention are clear so your pony can make sense of what you are asking.

think
like a pony
on the ground

8. When he walks, allow him to walk forward. If he thinks he should stop, show him, with a feel on the halter, that you would like him to keep walking forward on the circle.

If you have had to make the circle smaller to get him to listen to the backward feel of the rope then encourage him gently back out and away from you.

If you encourage him too quickly or with high phases of rhythm he may trot. This may cause him to be confused, thinking he has done something wrong.

9. When he is back on the circle away from you make sure you are turning with him.

Lift the hand nearest his head, the one holding the rope attached to the halter, and ask him to trot. If he does not listen, go through your phases of rhythmic pressure to signal and to encourage him to follow the feel of the rope on the halter.

10. When he is trotting, make sure that you turn with him and ask him to keep his nose on a circle as you did before.

11. When he tries to keep his nose on a circle, ask him to walk by sliding your hand away from his head down the rope to give him a backward feel. Repeat any signals or phases you need to show him what you want him to do.

12. Keep practising until he understands what you are asking him to do.

Reward him when he understands that backward pressure means slow down, forward pressure means go forward.

Repeat the exercises asking your pony to go to the left.

He should soon be able to:

1. Go forward on a circle.
2. Keep his nose on a circle.
3. Follow a feel to go forward into trot.
4. Keep out on a circle.
5. Go forward to walk.
6. Turn to face you.

When you and your pony can confidently do these exercises you will be helping him to relax, be supple and confident to follow his nose.

REMEMBER to be consistent in the way you ask your pony to do these exercises. You must make your intentions, body language and signals the same each time.

This way he can make sense of what you are asking of him.

By now your pony will be getting used to your body language and feel. He is starting to understand what you are asking of him.

You must be consistent and try to repeat the same body language and the same feel each time you ask. Always be as light and gentle as possible with your feel and as firm as necessary.

This way he can learn to follow your feel and your body language. If you change your body language and feel each time you talk to him, he may give you an answer you did not expect or want. He may start to ignore you because he cannot make sense of your language.

think
like a pony
on the ground

If you are consistent each time you ask him to look at you he will start to look for that signal.

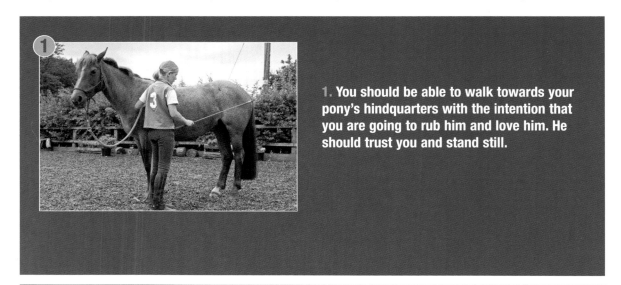

1. You should be able to walk towards your pony's hindquarters with the intention that you are going to rub him and love him. He should trust you and stand still.

2. You should be able to walk towards your pony's hindquarters with the intention that he moves away from you. He should feel your intention and move away. If he does not move you will give him a signal.

He has read your first body language signal and understood your intention.

Very soon your pony reads your intention before he reads your body language. He starts to know what you are thinking.

REMEMBER! **You must always be aware of your intention and body language as your pony is trying to understand what you are thinking and asking him to do.**

If your pony finds any of these exercises difficult, you may need to walk a small circle while he is moving on a bigger circle. This way you are making the circle easier for him to move forward on.

Make sure you do not walk backwards. This invites him to you, making the circle smaller.

Cantering on a small circle is very difficult. If your pony canters, try to ask him to trot. If he will not trot, you will have to walk with him until he can. This may need the help of your parent or guardian. If he wants to canter it may be because he is finding trotting difficult – he may be unbalanced or afraid. If this keeps happening seek professional help.

Canter work will be covered in a later workbook.

Chapter 6
Leading your pony from his shoulder

To be able to lead your pony you first have to be a good leader for him.

You are now starting to understand what being a good leader means.

You can now use your intention, feel and body language to ask your pony to:

1. Respect your personal space.
2. Allow you to touch him.
3. Move his feet.

You are learning to listen to what your pony is trying to say to you and to respond to him so that you can build a friendship based on respect and trust.

When you are a good leader for your pony then he will be willing to follow you.

A good leader makes a pony feel safe!

You have learned to ask your pony to follow you and to stop, respecting your personal space.

Now you are going to ask your pony to allow you to lead him forward from his shoulder, respect your personal space and allow you to walk with him.

From this position you can use your intention and body language to ask him to go where you go and to respect your personal space.

think
like a pony
on the ground

Exercise 12 – Asking your pony to follow your lead and walk with you

With adult supervision, in a safe place where you and your pony both feel comfortable, put the halter on and have the rope attached.

1. Stand at the side of your pony by his shoulder in line with his front legs. Face forwards, your feet and belly button pointing the same way as your pony.

Stand with your pony on your right side. Hold the rope attached to the halter in your left hand about an arm's length from the snap. Hold the free end of the rope in your other hand about an arm's length from the end.

Be relaxed!

2. Give your pony a friendly rub. Now have the intention that you would like to walk forward. Imagine your pony coming with you.

3. Offer your arm holding the rope attached to the halter forward.

Rock your body forward then take a step forward. Allow your pony to feel and see all these signals.

4. If he follows and walks with you, rub him as you walk and tell him he is a good boy. As you walk, make sure that there is space between you so he can see you and is aware of you.

5. If he does not follow and walk with you, you can encourage him by putting rhythmic pressure behind the drive line.

Put your hand holding the free end of the rope behind you and tap your pony either with your hand or the end of the rope.

He will see and feel this signal and should walk forward.

When he does, put your hand back by your side and rub him as you walk together. Tell him he is a good boy.

6. If he still does not walk forward with you, ask your parent or guardian to gently tap him on his bottom to encourage him forward. Make sure that they tap with rhythm and stop tapping the second he tries to walk forward. As they tap make sure you show your pony that you want him to walk with you by holding your intention, feel and body language.

7. In this position, at his shoulder, walk forwards. You are going to ask your pony to follow your intention, feel and body language and go where you go.

Exercise 13 – Changing direction with your pony

When you change direction you want your pony to feel your intention, see your body language and change direction with you.

1. As you walk, start to look towards your pony, and turn your shoulders and belly button towards your pony. This is just like the mare moving her foal.

2. This shows your pony that you want to walk in a different direction. So that you can move in a different direction your pony must first move out of your way. Have the intention that you are going to walk through your pony's front end and you would like him to turn and walk out of your way.

3. Start to walk where your eyes, shoulders and belly button are facing.

If your pony does not follow your lead and does not change direction with you, put your hands out in front of you. If he ignores this first signal, stretch out your arms.

If he ignores this signal, move your hands with rhythm towards his head.

If he ignores this signal, be willing to touch him with rhythm.

think
like a pony
on the ground

4. The second that he moves out of your way, look straight ahead with your eyes, shoulders and belly button.

He will feel and see that you are now walking in a different direction and he should turn and walk with you.

Make sure that you are relaxed but your body language is positive and clear. Look where you intend to go. This way your pony will be confident to walk with you and follow your lead.

5. If he walks in front of you, he is trying to out-manoeuvre you and be the leader. He is trying to get you to follow him. You can use a backward feel on the halter to ask him to step back. You can ask your parent or guardian to help you. This way your pony will get a stronger body language signal. You can go to exercise 15, on using your stick to make your body language signals bigger.

6. Keep walking forwards with eyes, shoulders and belly button facing forwards.

Now think about looking away from your pony. Turn your head and look where you want to walk. Start to turn your shoulders and belly button to face the new direction you want to move in.

Start to move in your new direction. If your pony comes with you, keep walking and rub him; tell him he is a good boy. Now look straight ahead with your eyes and belly button and keep walking.

7. If your pony does not follow your lead then lift your hand holding the rope and point to where you want him to go. This will let him feel and see where you intend to move. As soon as he moves with you, lower your hand and look forward in the new direction you are moving in. Tell him he is a good boy.

think
like a pony
on the ground

8. If he falls behind you, encourage him forward by putting your free hand behind you, behind his drive line. Use rhythm from your hand or rope to encourage him forward to walk next to you.

Exercise 14 – Asking your pony to stop with you

1. Walk with your pony, keeping your position at his shoulder. Look where you are going with your eyes, shoulders and belly button.

2. Start to think about stopping and have the intention that your pony will stop with you. When you have set your intention start to slow down your walk.

If your pony starts to slow down with you, think about stopping, then stop. If your pony stops with you and you are still at his shoulder give him a big rub and make a fuss of him.

3. If your pony does not slow down with you, then lift up your hand that is holding the rope attached to the halter. You may need to swap hands and shorten the rope a little.

With a steady feel from your hand, start to put backward pressure on the rope; your pony will feel this and should start to slow down.

think
like a pony
on the ground

If he slows down, then you think about stopping, then stop. If your pony stops with you still at his shoulder give him a big rub and make a fuss of him.

4. If he does not slow down with you he will start to try to walk in front of you. Lift up your hand holding the free end of the rope and hold it straight out in front of you. This will give a signal to your pony that you did not want him to come in front of you.

You may need to increase your signal by putting rhythm into your arm and directing it toward your pony's nose.

As soon as he tries to walk straight, ask him again to stop. Use a feel on the rope and make sure you are slowing down and thinking of stopping.

When he stops, make a fuss of him. If you are not at his shoulder do not worry. With practice you will be able to walk together.

When you have completed the exercise from one side of your pony try it from the other side.

Exercise 15 – Using a stick to make your body language clearer

If your pony finds any part of the previous exercises difficult or confusing then using a stick to make your body language bigger and clearer will help him to understand what you want.

Try this exercise with your pony even if he finds walking with you easy.

1. Before you start, make sure that your pony is comfortable with the stick and you can touch him all over with it.

You can loop the free end of your rope around your pony where his neck meets his withers.

think
like a pony
on the ground

2. Hold the rope at arm's length from the halter in your right hand. Hold your stick in your free hand.

You are going to use the stick as an extension of your own arm.

3. If you want to encourage him forward put the stick behind you and behind your pony's drive line.

4. Make sure you move the stick slowly with phases of rhythm. Touch the ground behind you and his drive line before you touch your pony.

5. If you need to, lift up your hand and stick to ask him to turn away with you. Be careful not to move too quickly. Let him see the stick lifting and signal him to move away. First lift the stick out with a straight arm, then take it slowly towards his front end.

6. You do not have to walk far with your pony – turn, walk, turn, walk, then reward him.

When you are both confident and comfortable walk further and turn more often. You can even take him for a short walk changing direction often.

This is a nice way to spend time together.

If your pony finds it dificult to walk in a straight line next to you and turn with you then:

Use a fence, wall or barrier to help keep him straight.

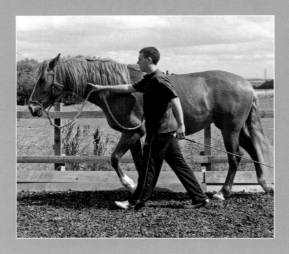
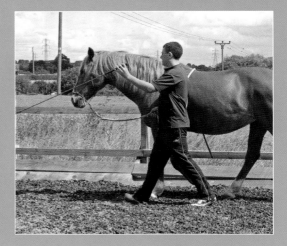

Ask him to walk with you, keeping at his shoulder, then ask him to stop.

Ask him to walk with you away from the fence, wall or barrier.

think
like a pony
on the ground

Ask him to walk back with you to the fence, wall or barrier.

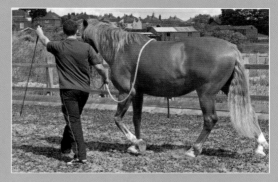

When you can do this you can ask him to walk with you anywhere at his shoulder.

What if your pony wants to stop and eat?

Sometimes all your pony can think about is his tummy. He may decide to take the lead and take you for a walk.

He may pull you where he wants to go.

If this happens there is no point trying to pull him as this will just make him try to pull you more.

think
like a pony
on the ground

You are going to unbalance your pony and walk backwards, encouraging him to turn his nose and follow the feel of the rope.

You may need to allow the rope to slip through your hands until you are at the end of it.

Make sure you are away from your pony's body so he can see and feel you. In this position he will best be able to follow the feel of the rope, turn his nose out and follow with his feet.

As soon as your pony follows you, gather up the rope. When he comes with you give him a rub and continue to lead him where you want.

In your pony does not follow your feel, try to step further away from him.

If he still does not come, you may need to ask a friend to tap his bottom with rhythm to encourage him to move forward. Keep walking backwards as your helper taps his bottom.

As soon as he moves make sure that your friend stops tapping and that you walk backwards gathering up the rope. When he comes to you give him a rub and continue to lead him.

When you can walk at your pony's side and ask him to follow you and stop when you do, then you are ready to ask him to walk backwards with you.

think
like a pony
on the ground

Exercise 16 – Asking your pony to walk backwards with you at his side

When you stop with your pony at your side, have the intention that you would like him to walk backwards with you.

1. Suggest with your body language that you are going backwards. Keep your feet still and sway a little backwards. If he moves backwards, stop and give him a rub.

2. If he does not move backwards, lift the hand that is holding the rope up and backwards. This will put a gentle backwards feel on the fiador knot. If your pony moves backwards, stop and give him a rub.

3. If he does not respond to your body language and feel on the fiador knot then use your leg, rope or stick to put rhythmic signals of pressure in front of your pony.

Use phases of pressure, always starting small and building up.

Your pony may not expect you to ask him to back up while you are standing in this position. You may need to make your body language clearer by using a stick.

As soon as he takes a step backwards, stop the rhythmic pressure and give him a rub.

You will soon be able to build a little routine:

1. Walk with me.
2. Turn with me.
3. Walk backwards with me.

You can use this routine whenever you are leading your pony, taking him for a walk or negotiating obstacles.

Chapter 7
Moving calmly through narrow spaces

You can now use the leadership and trust that you have built up to introduce your pony to new obstacles and situations.

You can help him to think and make sense of his world and understand what is expected of him.

Even if your pony is familiar with an obstacle or situation he may not be thinking or behaving in a calm, positive manner.

He may over-react to a situation and because he is not thinking he may scare himself or you. This can happen on the ground, when you are leading him or when you ride him.

Why would a pony be afraid of small, tight or narrow spaces?

From reading the 'Think like a Pony' foundation book you understand that a wild pony would avoid being cornered or trapped in a tight space. In a small space he cannot run away from a predator. If a predator could trap him in a tight space he would be an easy target.

All ponies are therefore naturally suspicious of small spaces because their movement is restricted. This could be a:
1. Stable.
2. Narrow gateway.
3. Narrow gap.
4. Trailer or horsebox.

think
like a pony
on the ground

Some ponies do not feel safe walking along a fence or a hedge line!

You are going to use all the skills you have learned so far to help your pony to learn that he can feel safe in these situations. With any pony, even one who is confident, there is a safe way for you to ask him to move his feet.

A way that is safe for you and your pony.

A stable is a small space for a pony that is meant to live in a wide-open space. Sometimes a pony may find going in and out of a stable a thing that may cause him to act out of fear.

He may find:

1. The doorway of the stable too narrow or too low.

2. His stable too small or dark (he prefers the wide-open space of the field).

3. He does not like it when he is left in his stable while his other pony friends are out in the paddock.

think
like a pony
on the ground

To keep you and your pony safe when you are leading him in and out of his stable, he must understand some simple rules.

1. Please do not barge into my personal space.
2. Please put your feet where I am asking you to put them.

These are leadership issues.

REMEMBER! **You must be a good leader for your pony and have clear intentions of what you want to achieve together.**

If you do not have a stable for your pony you will still need to learn to lead him in and out of small spaces safely. Use your imagination to create a small space that you can use for practising. For example, jump wings, poles or any safe obstacle could mark out a pretend stable or small space.

Even if your pony is polite and well mannered when going in and out of his stable, make sure you do this exercise. It is IMPORTANT **to lead him in and out of his stable correctly.**

think
like a pony
on the ground

Exercise 17 – Leading your pony in and out of a stable safely

With adult supervision, in a safe place where you and your pony both feel comfortable, put the halter on your pony and have the rope attached.

1. Stand at your pony's shoulder and lead your pony towards his stable door and stop outside.

2. Rub your pony and let him relax. Hold the rope attached to the halter about an arm's length from the snap with the rest of the rope over your arm.

3. If possible open your stable door. If not, ask your adult helper to do it for you.

4. Stand at the side of the open door outside the stable and look inside. Have the intention that you want your pony to walk into his stable.

5. Lift the hand holding the rope and point into the stable. This will give your pony a feel on the halter to go forward into the stable.

6. Make sure you are not in his way and that he can move forward. Keep your hands soft and as open as possible on the rope. As your pony moves forward, allow the rope to slip through your hand to allow him to move.

think
like a pony
on the ground

7. Stay outside of the stable and allow your pony to walk into his stable. With a gentle feel on the rope ask your pony to turn and face you.

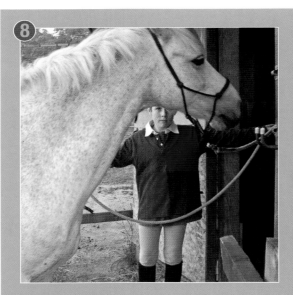

8. If your pony does not follow your intention and feel into his stable then lift up your free hand. Direct your hand behind his drive line encouraging him forward. If you need to increase your phases of pressure to encourage him to move, do so slowly and politely, stopping as soon as he moves forward. If you need to, you can use your rope to move him forwards. As he starts to walk forward put down your free hand. This lets him know he is doing the correct thing.

Allow the rope to slip through your hand so he can move. When he is in the stable, gently close your hand around the rope so he can feel the pressure. This encourages him to turn to face you.

think
like a pony
on the ground

9. You are now outside the stable and your pony is inside the stable looking at you.

10. You can now go into the stable with your pony. If he is in the doorway ask him politely to back up out of your way. You can use steady pressure or rhythmic signals of pressure to do this.

11. You can now close the door and take off his halter.

Leading out of the stable

1. Place the halter on your pony with the rope attached. Make sure you are polite.

2. Open the door but do not step out. Rub your pony to help him to relax.

3. Look out of the door to show your pony that is where you want him to go.

4. If he does not step forward, lift your hand holding the rope and point to the open door.

5. When he steps forward, allow the rope to move through your hand so your pony feels he is allowed to move.

6. If your pony does not move forward out of his stable you may need to lift your free hand and direct rhythmic pressure behind his drive line. This will encourage him forward. If you need to, slowly increase your signals of rhythmic pressure. You may need to use your rope with rhythm.

As soon as he moves forward put down your free hand. This lets your pony know he has done the correct thing.

think
like a pony
on the ground

7. Stay inside the stable and when your pony is outside, slowly close your hand around the rope. He will feel that you want him to stop and turn to face you.

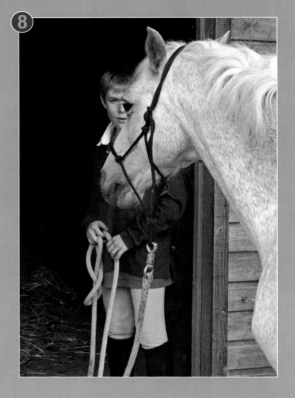

8. When he stops, walk out of the stable and rub him. Close the door.

You have both respected one another's space and managed to go in and out of the stable safely.

What if your pony runs out of his stable and pulls away from you?

Sometimes a pony will run out of his stable with no intention of stopping, even if you are holding the rope attached to the halter.

Try to understand why your pony may do this. He may be:

A. Afraid of being left alone in his stable and wants to be with other ponies.

B. In a hurry to escape from his stable, back to the open space of the paddock.

C. Afraid of passing through the stable doorway; he may think the gap is too small.

Any or all of the above could be reasons why a pony runs out of his stable. He has to learn that there is no need to be afraid, before this becomes a habit. Habits are often difficult to break.

If your pony runs out of his stable you must make sure he is not afraid and help him to think.

A. You need your pony to think about following the feel of the rope and halter and turning to face you.

B. You need him to think about turning to face you and not running away. By turning to face you he can learn about facing the 'fear of the situation'. The gap is really not that scary!

You are going to use one of the edges of the frame of your stable doorway to help you to turn your pony.

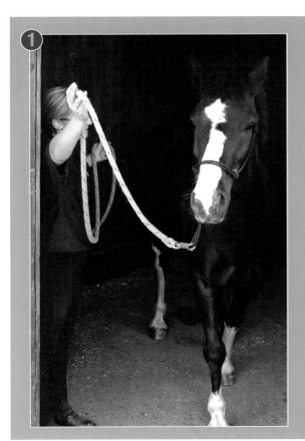

You will need adult help for this!

With your pony in the stable, have the halter on and the rope attached. You may need your adult helper to stand behind you to hold the end of the rope for you.

1. Stand to one side of the door frame as shown in the picture.

think
like a pony
on the ground

If it is safe, open the door or ask your helper to open it.

2. Ask your pony to step out of the stable. Allow the rope to slip a little so he can move out of the stable.

3. As he takes up the rope to move out of the stable and run, close your fingers around the rope, lean back so that the frame acts as extra leverage and support to turn your pony.

You may need to repeat this process more than once so your pony learns there is no need to run away and indeed that he cannot run away.

Some ponies feel that they need to rush through small spaces. A pony may be comfortable with his own stable doorway but tense when asked to go through a strange gateway or small opening.

If you ride your pony out on a hack/trail ride you may need to open a gate, go through it and then turn to close a gate. This can be dangerous if your pony is not confident with the procedure. He may rush or make it difficult for you to move him.

It is your job to help your pony to approach a gate confidently and to step through it slowly, and then to turn to fasten the gate.

Preparation for riding through gates starts on the ground, then you can both be safe.

think
like a pony
on the ground

Exercise 18 – Guiding your pony through a gate

With adult supervision, in a safe place where you and your pony both feel comfortable, have the halter on your pony and the rope attached.

1. Lead your pony to a closed gate.

If your pony rushes through gates or runs away, begin with a wide gate. Later on, as you both gain confidence, find a smaller gate or mark out an imaginary one.

Make sure you do this exercise slowly so that you have a chance to improve your skills and understanding of how to ask your pony to move up to and through a gate.

2. Ask your pony to stand and face the gate. You should stand on the side of your pony that allows you easily to open the gate.

3. Ask your pony to back up using steady or rhythmic signals of pressure – it does not matter which type – then open the gate.

4. Ask him to move forward again.

5. Keep hold of the lead rope attached to the halter and ask your pony to step through the gate. You should stay on the other side of the gate.

think
like a pony
on the ground

6. If your pony does not move forward, with your free hand direct rhythmic pressure behind his drive line. You could use rhythm from your hand or the rope. Build your rhythm slowly and stop the minute your pony walks forward. This way he knows he has done the correct thing.

7. With a feel on the rope ask your pony to turn to face you and the gate. When he stops and looks at you and the gate, you can step through and ask him to follow you.

8. Ask your pony to take a step backward away from the gate. Make sure you maintain your position.

Practise in different situations. Some gates open towards you, and some away from you. Your rope will allow you to manoeuvre your pony and keep yourself safe.

think
like a pony
on the ground

Sometimes it is not safe to go through a gate with your pony:

If, for instance, you are putting your pony into a paddock with other ponies, it may be safer for you to stay outside the paddock and not follow him through the gate.

Other ponies in the paddock may act in a way that makes it unsafe for you to enter. They may gather around the gate making it difficult for you to go in.

Your pony may be in the habit of running from the gate and 'kicking up' as he leaves. This can be very dangerous and he may accidentally kick you.

Other ponies may frighten you or your pony. If they frighten your pony he may defend himself and kick out.

think
like a pony
on the ground

The gateway may be muddy and there may be a risk you could slip.

If for any reason it is not safe for you to go through the gate with your pony then you can ask him to go forward through the gate and, once he is in the paddock, you can take his halter off over the gate.

Preparing your pony to walk through and into small spaces

This is preparation for walking into any confined or small/restricted space where a pony may feel trapped, such as a trailer or horsebox. This is also like the starting stalls for a racehorse. By starting simply, you can build your pony's confidence and trust in you and the obstacle. As he grows in confidence and you can make the 'tunnel' more challenging, so he can learn more about his environment.

Exercise 19 – Asking your pony to walk through a pole 'tunnel'

With adult supervision, in a safe place where you and your pony both feel comfortable, put the halter on your pony and have the rope attached.

1. Make a 'tunnel' with two poles and blocks (or similar safe objects).

Make sure the path is wide enough for your pony to walk through comfortably.

2. Stand outside the 'tunnel' at the 'entrance' with your focus on the entrance to the 'tunnel'.

3. Keep your feet still and ask your pony to stand at the entrance to the tunnel. You can use either steady pressure or rhythmic pressure to ask your pony to move his feet into position.

It is IMPORTANT that you try to keep your feet in one spot!

If you need to, you can use a stick to make your body language bigger so you can better direct your pony.

4. When your pony is comfortable standing at the entrance to the tunnel turn your focus (eyes, belly button and feet) along the 'tunnel'.

Imagine your pony walking up the 'tunnel' – this sets your intention.

With a soft feel on the rope ask your pony to walk forward into the 'tunnel'.

5. If he is comfortable doing this he will not hesitate and will be calm. Walk with him and allow him to walk through the 'tunnel' and out the other side.

6. If he finds this safe and comfortable then you can start to make the tunnel more challenging. Here are some ideas: put a coat or blanket over the poles or simply raise them.

REMEMBER! If at any time your pony appears scared or worried, slow down and reward his slightest try. Allow him time to learn from the situation.

If your pony does not want to walk through the pole tunnel:

Start to build up his confidence by placing the poles on the ground and asking him to walk through. If he is unwilling, ask with a soft feel on the rope and gently encourage him with rhythmic signals of pressure behind the drive line as you have before.

think
like a pony
on the ground

Look for signs that he is relaxing and reward the slightest try to move forward.

Build his confidence slowly.

As his confidence grows, raise one end of the 'tunnel' but make sure it is wide and friendly looking. Ask him to move through it. Once he is happy with this, raise the other end of the 'tunnel'.

Be patient but determined to help him to gain confidence.

You may need to repeat the exercise several times.

You can use the 'tunnel' to build your pony's confidence so he feels safer in small or tight spaces.

When he is confident, ask him to walk backwards in the 'tunnel'.

When your pony is in the pole 'tunnel' ask him to drop his head with a slight backward feel on his halter, and ask him to take one step back. When he does, reward him and ask him to walk forwards.

Build up the amount of backward steps you ask for.

Eventually you will be able to back him through the 'tunnel'.

You can stand in front of your pony or at the side of him. What is important is your focus and intention.

If he wobbles and knocks a pole down, don't worry. If he scares himself, go back to walking through the tunnel. Start again and check your focus and intention. Take your time – 'one step at a time'.

As he gains confidence ask him to stop in the 'tunnel'. Then raise the poles.

You can make the tunnel narrower to challenge your pony and help him to learn about small spaces.

Exercise 20 – Ask your pony to walk between a fence (or wall or hedge) and an obstacle

This is like the pole 'tunnel' but because one of the sides is solid it appears smaller or tighter to your pony. This situation offers a greater challenge and learning experience for your pony.

With adult supervision, in a safe place where you and your pony both feel comfortable, put the halter on your pony and have the rope attached.

1. Set up an obstacle along the side of a fence (hedge or wall); make sure the gap is nice and wide.

2. Stand facing the entrance to the obstacle, with your pony waiting for your direction.

3. Put your focus and intention on your pony walking between the obstacle and the fence, hedge or wall.

4. With the hand holding the rope attached to the halter use a soft feel and ask your pony forward.

5. If he is happy and willing to keep going, allow him through the gap.

6. Once through, look at his hindquarters and ask him to stop and turn to face you. Give him a rub and make a fuss of him and repeat the other way.

7. If he is unsure at all, make the obstacle simpler, ask only for one step and reward him. Invite him through step by step. If he rushes through, don't worry, just widen the gap. As his confidence grows he will learn there is no need to rush.

8. If he appears scared or nervous, widen the gap or make the obstacle smaller.

If he pulls back and appears very scared, seek professional help.

REMEMBER! Start small and build up his confidence.
Reward every small try and look for signs of him relaxing.

Repeat the exercise until he is comfortable and confident and he has learned from the situation. Give him lots of praise and rubs.

Sometimes a pony may take a long time to make these small steps. Be prepared for one step today and one step tomorrow.

Help him to build confidence in you and confidence in himself.

Build up these exercises so he can follow you and back up in the obstacle.

Chapter 8
Stepping over obstacles

Ponies need to understand the world around them. They need to learn what is safe and what is unsafe.

They need to learn what will or won't harm them and what they can play with.

REMEMBER! **By being curious the foal learns to be brave.**

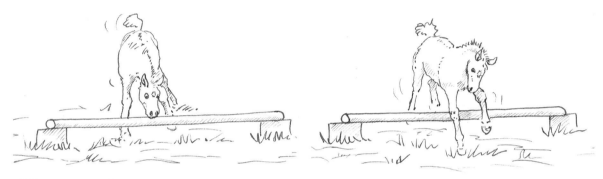

When you ask your pony to move towards, through, or over an obstacle you are helping him to:

1. Learn, by investigating new objects and situations.
2. Be confident and brave when approaching new objects and situations.
3. Have trust in you and what you are asking him to do.

When you are asking your pony to move towards, around or over a new obstacle, it is very important you remember to see the world through his eyes.

REMEMBER!
You are not scared of the same things.

You must allow him to take his time so he can THINK.

You must reward his slightest try when he does what you are asking him to do.

You may think a pole on the ground or a plastic jump is nothing to be afraid of.

If your pony acts afraid or is suspicious, respect his feelings but be determined to help him to understand the situation and learn from it.

Before you ask your pony to deal with any new obstacle you must have worked successfully through all the exercises so far.

You must be confident with the exercises and developing your horsemanship skills.

This means knowing when to ask your pony to do something, when to stop asking and when to reward.

By now, you and your pony should be understanding and trusting each other.

If you do not feel confident with your pony in any way, seek professional help before attempting the following tasks.

You are going to start with a simple and familiar obstacle – a pole on the ground.

If you do not have a pole you can use a log or plank of wood. Make sure that your obstacle is safe, simple and on the ground.

Exercise 21 – Asking your pony to follow you over a pole

With adult supervision, in a safe place where you and your pony both feel comfortable, put the halter on your pony and have the rope attached.

1. Place a pole on the floor.

think
like a pony
on the ground

2. With your pony following you, confidently walk towards the pole.

3. If your pony is following you confidently and you can feel that he is not hesitating, walk over the pole.

4. When your pony has followed you and walked over the pole let him know with your body language that you are going to stop. Ask him to stop behind you.

When you want to stop, slow down, then stop. Make sure he can read your body language at all times so he is not confused about your intentions. If you stop suddenly he will be shocked and may act shocked.

think
like a pony
on the ground

5. If you feel a pull on the rope attached to the halter, slow down your walk. Imagine that as you feel the pull you are going to change direction. It does not matter if you go left or right.

If you cross the pole and your pony still resists (it will feel like he does not want to follow you), change direction. This will unbalance him so he feels that he has to follow.

think
like a pony
on the ground

When he does, stop and make a fuss of him.

Repeat the exercise until he follows you with no resistance.

When you have both stopped, turn around and rub him.

If your pony appears scared or suspicious, walk around the pole. As he shows signs of relaxing walk closer to the pole until you can stop near to it. When he appears more confident ask him to follow you over it.

If your pony pulls away or runs backwards away from the pole, seek professional help.

Once confident, repeat this several times.

If your pony follows you easily and stops outside your personal space, try running over the pole so he can trot behind you.

To build your pony's confidence it is important that he can approach obstacles on his own and gain experience for himself.

Exercise 22 – Asking your pony to go over the pole on his own

1. Stand at the end of your pole. Hold the rope attached to the halter in one hand about an arm's length from the snap, the rest of the rope in the other hand about an arm's length from the end.

2. Using a feel on the rope ask your pony to stand and face the pole.

You may need to use rhythmic pressure to ask him to back away from you a little.

3. You want your pony to stand in front of the pole and wait.

think
like a pony
on the ground

If he does not understand and walks over the pole it does not matter. Just try again until he can stand in front of the pole.

Sometimes this takes several tries, so be patient.

4. When he stands in front of the pole ask him to walk forward. Direct him with a steady feel on the rope attached to the halter. Put your focus and intention on him walking over the pole. Look where you want him to step.

5. Allow him to walk over the pole.

6. When he has successfully walked over the pole ask him to turn to face you. Run your hand lightly down the rope making sure you do not pull him towards you. At the same time walk towards his hindquarters. If you need to, use signals of rhythmic pressure towards his hindquarters to ask him to turn and face you.

Give him a rub.

7. Repeat the exercise in the opposite direction.

What if your pony is afraid of the pole?

Your pony may follow you over a pole but will not walk over it on his own. He needs to build his confidence in himself.

think
like a pony
on the ground

If your pony's body language shows you that he is afraid of the pole you MUST SLOW DOWN.

1. When you ask him forward, look for the slightest try that he is thinking of moving forward. He may only lean his body slightly, drop his head or tip his ear. When you see any sign that looks like he is thinking about going toward the pole, stop asking.

If he is convinced that the pole is going to hurt him, you may need to go back to leading him across the pole, then ask again.

2. Stand at the end of the pole and ask him forward with the hand holding the rope. Make sure your focus is where you want him to go. If he does not try to move forward or think about moving forward you are going to have to make your body language bigger.

When your pony can see that your body language has changed he will better understand your intention.

You intend to ask him toward the pole so that he can see for himself that it will not hurt him.

think
like a pony
on the ground

3. Lift the arm holding the free end of the rope straight out away from your body.

Keep a steady feel on the halter asking him forward.

If he steps or tries to step forward, lower your hands and stop asking him forward.

This way your pony is rewarded for trying and he knows you will not force him over the pole.

4. If he does not move forward you may need to move your free arm with rhythm to encourage him to move forward. Direct your rhythm behind his drive line.

REMEMBER that rhythm behind the drive line will encourage him forward.

Make sure:

1. You keep the feel on the halter to go forward.
2. You do not pull him forward.
3. You keep looking where you want him to go.
4. You don't change your focus, or he will be confused and won't understand where you want him to go.
5. Your signals start slow and build up slowly.

You can twirl your arm or tap it against your leg. You can lift your rope and twirl or swing.

It does not matter as long as you keep your focus and keep your steady feel on the halter. Use your signals of rhythmic pressure to encourage him forward. If he trots forward that is ok. Repeat the exercise until he can walk.

think
like a pony
on the ground

The moment he tries to walk, stop asking.

Keep repeating the process until he can put his head over the pole then his feet.

If he rushes, do not worry. He may still think the pole might 'grab him'!

If your pony can easily and confidently do these simple exercises, see if you can:

1. Ask him, using steady pressure, to stop over the pole.
2. Stop with one foot over the pole.
3. Step back with his front feet over the pole.
4. Step backwards with his back feet over the pole.

It will take time to build up his confidence and trust so be patient.

If he runs backwards, seek professional help.

think
like a pony
on the ground

Raising the pole

When your pony can confidently walk over a pole when you ask him then you can get ready to ask him to go over a small jump. At first the jump must be small, even if your pony is used to jumping. Jumping on a rope is different and you must start small to build up his confidence and your timing. At first you want him to trot over a raised pole or small jump.

First you must be able to ask your pony to trot out on a circle then trot over a pole.

It is IMPORTANT that you practise this exercise without your pony before you do it together. To prepare for this:

Try this! Planning your route

1. Without your pony, put a pole on the ground with enough space around it for you to be able to ask your pony onto a circle a short distance away from the pole.

2. Imagine you have your pony on the end of your 10ft/3m line and he is trotting a circle around you but not over the pole.

think
like a pony
on the ground

3. As you turn with your pony you will see, with soft eyes, the pole come into your vision.

4. Imagine that at this point you will walk toward the pole and lead your pony over it. Imagine your pony trotting over it.

5. Imagine that after he has trotted over the pole you will ask him to stop and look at you.

If you want to you can ask a friend to be your imaginary pony.

Exercise 23 – Asking your pony to trot over a pole

When you understand the exercise you are ready to ask your pony to trot from a circle over a pole on the ground.

With adult supervision, in a safe place where you and your pony both feel comfortable, put the halter on your pony and have the rope attached.

1. Stand in front of your pony and give him a friendly rub.

2. Ask him to step back and step out onto a circle to the right.

3. Turn with him and when you are both ready ask him to trot.

4. When he has trotted around you once or twice start to look for the pole on the ground.

5. Imagine your pony is going to trot over the pole. Walk towards the pole and lead your pony over it so he can trot over it.

6. When he has trotted over the pole, slide your hand holding the rope attached to the halter lightly towards your pony. Keep your hands soft. Make sure you do not pull him. At the same time walk toward your pony's hindquarters and ask him to stop and look at you.

It is IMPORTANT to keep imagining your pony doing what you are asking him to do. This way your intentions stay clear and positive.

If you find it difficult to find the timing and place to lead your pony over a pole from the circle, it does not matter.

You just need to practise with or without your pony.

You will soon find the place and time to ask your pony to follow your feel over the pole.

When you can confidently do this to the right, repeat the exercise to the left.

When you can ask your pony to trot over a pole to the left and the right then you are ready to ask him to trot over a raised pole.

Exercise 24 – Asking your pony over a raised pole

Raise the pole to make a small jump, circle your pony in trot then lead him to the jump and ask him to trot over it. When he has jumped the raised pole, ask him to look at you and make a big fuss of him.

If your pony can trot over a raised pole it tells you many things about his attitude to the pole and jumping.

If he calmly trots over the pole and he does not change his rhythm, he is confident about what he is doing.

If he changes the rhythm of his trot and speeds up, he is rushing and is afraid or unsure. He may feel he needs to rush over the jump to escape or he may feel unbalanced trotting over the pole.

If he leaps over the pole he may not be sure how to tackle this obstacle safely. He may not be sure what to do with his legs! He may want to put a safe distance between himself and the pole in case it may hurt him or catch him. He may need time to learn how to confidently trot over a raised pole.

If he stops in front of the pole he may be afraid or unsure how to tackle it.

REMEMBER! **A wild pony will protect his legs at all costs.**

think
like a pony
on the ground

If your pony will not trot over the raised pole:

1. If he does not want to go forward, raise the arm holding the free end of the rope to signal to him you want him to go forward. Make sure your feel on the rope attached to the halter is asking him forward and not pulling him.

You may need to increase the rhythm or use your rope or stick.

If he appears afraid or anxious, go back to a pole on the ground. Then raise one side and eventually go back to a raised pole.

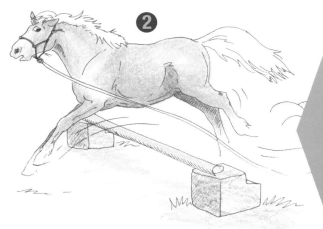

2. If he leaps, rushes or canters you will need to take the exercise slowly. You want him to understand he can trot over a raised pole. You are going to ask him to stop and look at you when you have seen an improvement in his attitude to the raised pole. He may lower his head, appear more relaxed or stop rushing.

If he is leaping don't make a fuss about it. When he leaps less, reward him by asking him to stop and look at you.

think
like a pony
on the ground

Eventually he will leap less and less and then not at all.

If he speeds up, don't worry. When you see him slowing down, trying to find his rhythm, reward him. Ask him to stop and look at you. Eventually he will be able to trot over the raised pole and not change his rhythm.

If he canters don't ask him to trot but reward him the moment he tries to trot over the pole. Eventually he will be able to trot over the raised pole without cantering.

When you are allowing your pony to sort out his attitude to trotting over a pole he may make a few or more circles.

You will have to move your feet and move with him to lead him over the pole.

You must not get in front of him because this may cause him to stop.

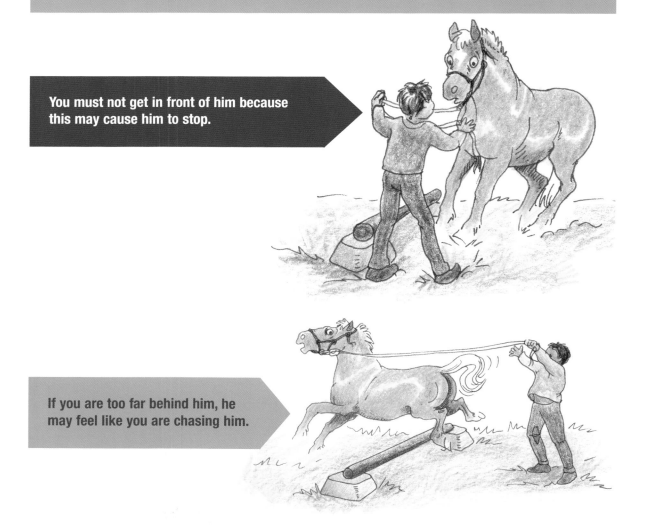

If you are too far behind him, he may feel like you are chasing him.

think
like a pony
on the ground

Stay at the end of the rope in line with his shoulder. This is the best position to give him a lead and a feel of what you are asking him to do. Keep your belly button, eyes and shoulders in line with the rope and your pony's head at all times.

If he finds this exercise scary and is taking a long time to find his rhythm to trot over the raised pole, go back to walking over a pole on a circle, then trot a pole on a circle, then raise one end of the pole, then raise the other end of the pole. When you are both confident with this exercise you can raise the pole a little more.

Make sure you raise the pole a little at a time and keep it below 2ft 6in/75cm. As the jump gets bigger your pony may need to canter over the jump. This is perfectly normal but he should not be rushing or running away from the jump.

If he starts to rush or leap, or look in anyway concerned, go back to a height he is confident with. Sometimes you need to go back to a pole on the ground. By asking your pony to jump on line (jump while you are holding the rope attached to the halter) you can see and learn how he jumps and where he takes off and lands.

You are helping him to build his confidence and his muscles. You are helping him to understand that he can safely go over the jump.

The confidence gained over these low poles will make your pony nicer and safer to ride, when you jump over any obstacle. So take time to practise! If he learns to be calm and keeps his rhythm over poles he will be calm and rhythmical over bigger jumps.

Jumping is very tiring. Taking off and landing over a jump can jar a pony's feet and body, so make sure the ground is not too hard or too slippery and that you do not over-tire your pony. Have fun! This is great preparation for your pony if you want to ride him over a jump.

Chapter 9
Introducing your pony to new things

You now have 'horsemanship' skills!

1. You know how to protect your personal space.
2. You know how to ask your pony to move his feet.
3. You know when to reward him.
4. You know when to use approach and retreat.

Ponies are naturally curious

You can start to introduce your pony to new objects or situations so that you can help him to build his confidence. You can encourage him to be naturally curious and discover for himself that objects are not scary or dangerous. Using simple leading techniques that you have learned, you could ask your pony to go forward to sniff a new object.

You must always make sure that you are SAFE and protect your personal space.

1. You might ask your pony to follow you.
2. Walk by his side.
3. Lead him forward on a circle.
4. You may do all three in that order, just as you have done before.

What is IMPORTANT is you use 'feel' to ask him. Allow him time to think and reward him often. Take your time and have fun!

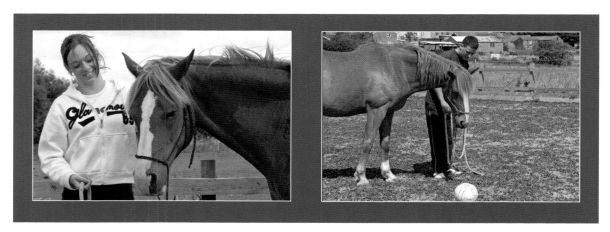

If your pony is scared or anxious about new objects, remember that ponies are naturally curious. See if you can get him to follow you – following the object. If he is worried, build his confidence in the object by approaching the object and retreating from it. Try to approach a little closer each time. This does not have to be done in one day or one session. If your pony is very scared you may need to build his confidence over several sessions.

REMEMBER: Reward him often when he tries to do the right thing or shows signs of being calm or brave.

He will soon start to become braver. He may even think he is moving the object and in charge!

You can build your pony's confidence in the things that you can touch him with and where you can touch him.

Always start small and build up. Use approach and retreat whenever you need to.
Allow your pony to see the object and offer him the chance to sniff it.
Be imaginative and have fun together!

If your pony is nervous or anxious whenever there is a sudden movement, help him to get used to it by introducing him to moving things slowly.

think
like a pony
on the ground

Try skipping around him or towards him. If he moves away retreat and slow down your movement, but do not stop – move with him. When he can stand still, reward him by giving him a rub and then standing still yourself.

Build up his confidence until you can skip up to him and around him.

You can move a flag on a stick around him, or introduce other interesting objects.

If he appears anxious allow him to move his feet and retreat by slowing down the movement of the object to a point where he can tolerate it. Build his confidence slowly.

Have fun!

When you are introducing your pony to new things, always be aware of his body language. Try to understand his concerns. What is he thinking?! What is he going to do? Is he learning from the situation?

think
like a pony
on the ground

If he looks at any time like he is going to fall asleep and shut you out, change what you are doing. Give him a scratch and wake him up or take him for a walk.

As you build your own skills and understanding you can help your pony to build his confidence and learn to be brave, then you will be safe together.

A confident pony is a thinking pony – a thinking pony is a safe pony!

Introducing your pony to strange noises

A strange noise may be a cause for concern for a wild pony. He must be alert to danger at all times. A strange noise could be a hissing snake or a growling lion. He can take no chances and may act on his instinct, feeling he may need to run at any moment.

Putting fly spray on your pony may be a difficult thing to do because the sound of the spray causes him to feel alarmed. Now that you understand why, you can use the horsemanship skills you have learned so far to help your pony understand that the fly spray will not hurt him.

You can:

1. Introduce the spray to him, ask him to be curious and sniff it.
2. Use approach and retreat with the spray.
3. Drift with him, allowing him to move his feet so that he does not feel trapped.
4. Reward his slightest try to be brave, to relax or to stand still.

REMEMBER! Letting your pony move his feet when he is scared allows him time to think.

If you try to ask your pony to stand still while he is scared and upset he will only think about moving. He is not being silly or stupid, stubborn or bad. He is just behaving like a pony who is scared.

Allowing him time to drift and move his feet gives him time to think and learn from the situation. This will show him that:

- the clippers,
- the fly spray, or
- the hosepipe… **will not kill him!**

He will learn through:

- Approach and retreat.
- Rewarding his slightest try to stand still or relax.
- Repeating the exercises… **that he can survive the situation.**

Introducing your pony to fly spray

Fly spray is expensive, so you could practise with water in a plant sprayer.

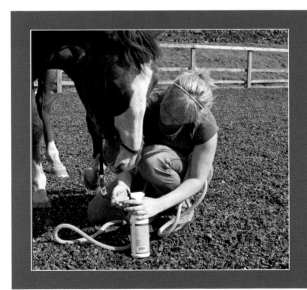

You might:
Ask him to sniff the bottle and introduce the smell of the spray on your hands.

think
like a pony
on the ground

Be prepared for him to move his feet. Keep hold of the rope loosely in one hand and move with him. Spray far enough away from him so that he can see and hear it but the spray does not touch him.

If he does not react, approach him with the spray. If he reacts, retreat from him. Look for signs that he is relaxing and thinking or attempting to stand still. As soon as he does, stop spraying and reward him, give him a rub and tell him he is a good boy. Build up his confidence until you get nearer and nearer and eventually spray him. Make sure that you do not stop spraying when he is upset and moving his feet.

Ask him to follow you and the spray, encouraging him to be curious. This lets him investigate the spray for himself. He will feel that he can work things out in his own time. He may feel that he is chasing the spray. When he can touch the spray or at least get very close to it, stop spraying. Let him think he can turn the spray off. As he follows you with the spray, he may lower his head and neck; this shows he is thinking and relaxing.

think
like a pony
on the ground

Try spraying your pony with water, fly spray or a soothing lavender wash.

Introducing your pony to clippers

Your pony may be afraid of the noise of the clippers or the vibration on his skin. Use something milder, like an electric toothbrush or a battery-operated shaver that you can hold in your hand, for the first introduction. Work with it in exactly the same way as you did when introducing your pony to fly spray.

When you can touch him with the toothbrush or shaver he may even enjoy a gentle massage with it on any tight muscles. When he is relaxed and confident with this you could let the clippers run and allow him to feel the vibration, without actually clipping his hair. Start on the large muscles of his shoulders before moving on to the rest of his body.

What you have learned so far

You are now able to direct your pony where you want on the ground. You can use any of the skills that you have learned so far to build your pony's confidence to tackle any obstacle.

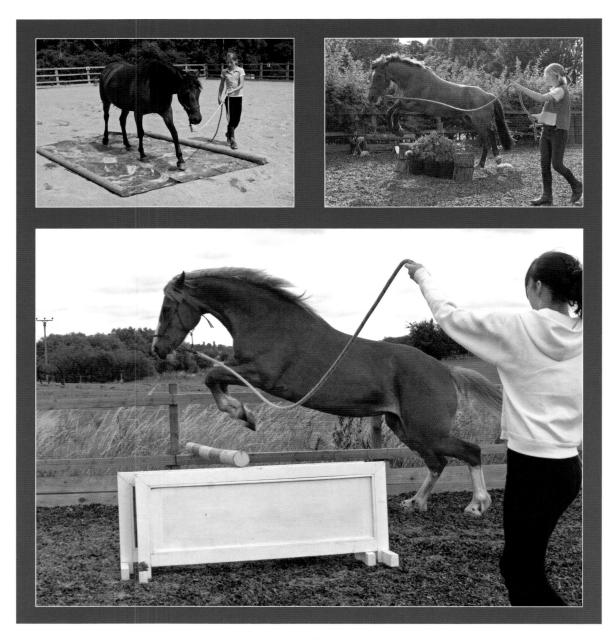

think
like a pony
on the ground

You have a communication with each other through:

1. Intention.
2. Body language.
3. Focus.
4. Steady pressure.
5. Rhythmic pressure.

You can use this communication in every situation when you are around your pony. You can now do many things with your pony, which make you interesting to be with.

This communication will keep you both safe and happy.

The exercises have prepared your pony to be confident and follow what you are asking him to do. Using the skill and understanding you have learned so far, you can make your pony's world easier for him to understand. You can help him to build up his confidence.

By allowing him time to think he can learn from situations.

By rewarding each try he makes, he doesn't feel rushed and he will learn.

think
like a pony
on the ground

By using approach and retreat you have helped to build your pony's confidence in your feel and what you are asking him to do.

By being consistent with your pony he can read your body language and understand what you are asking him to do.

By focusing your body language and intentions (thoughts) you are being responsible for your communication with your pony.

think
like a pony
on the ground

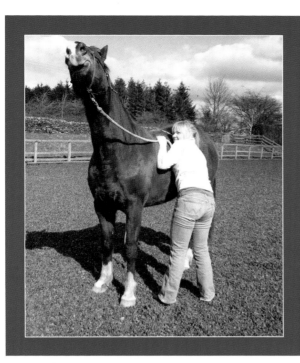

By loving and praising him you are letting him know that you care.

By respecting his bravery and his fears you are being a good friend.

As you both become willing partners together, you can do anything.

The ability to move your pony on the ground and establishing leadership is vital before you ride him.

If you want to have a good relationship with your pony when you are in the saddle then you must first have a good relationship with him on the ground.

think
like a pony
on the ground

If you want to ride your pony you must be able to ask him to follow your feel and move his feet where you want him to go. He needs to follow your intention and your feel when you are in the saddle.

You want to be able to ask him to move from a slight touch or feel of pressure. If he does not respond you will use rhythmic pressure to encourage him to follow your feel.

He learns this first with you on the ground.

What next?

In the next workbook, Think Like a Pony in the Saddle, you will learn how to apply all the skills you have learned so far when you ride your pony so that you can ask him to:

1. Trust you so that you can put a saddle on his back.
2. Go forward.
3. Stop.
4. Move his back end.
5. Move his front end.
6. Back up.
7. Ride a circle.
8. Move left.
9. Move right.
10. Negotiate obstacles.

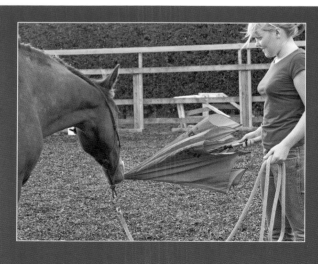

It is fun and safe when your pony is a willing friend and partner.

Have fun!

For further information and help, visit the THINK LIKE A PONY website:
www.lynnhenry.co.uk.

Notes

Notes

Notes

Notes

Notes